Gardening

Real: Climate

Change and

Rediscovering Food

Security With A

Home Garden

By Gaia Min

Table Of Contents

Table Of Contents — 2

Introduction - A Dynamic World — 5

Small Scale Gardening: A More Practical Way To Secure Food — 13

    Battling Drought: Amazing Abilities Of Mulch — 16

    Reducing Flood Damage: Raised Garden Beds — 18

    Wind Damage: Planting in the Proper Location — 20

    Disease and Pests: Polyculture and Organic Gardening — 23

    Chilling Hours and Erratic Freezes: Fruit Tree Dilemma — 27

    Relying on Large Farms is Risky — 32

Climate Adaptable Fruit Trees (and Shrubs) For Self-sufficiency — 34

    Figs — 38

    Grapes — 42

    Pomegranates — 46

    Jujube — 51

Persimmons	55
Owari Satsuma Mandarin Citrus	60
Self-pollinating Pecan	64
Fruit Trees Are Just The Beginning	68

Maintaining Food Security With a Short Growing Season   69

Polytunnels: The Cheaper Greenhouse	71
Benefits of a Polytunnel	76
Potatoes: The Survival Crop	80
Learning From Potato History	82

Exploring New Crops: The Usefulness Of Varieties and Foreign Plants   87

Ways to Find New Varieties to Grow	90
Thinking Outside The Box: Foreign Vegetables and Fruits	94

Lost Gardening Techniques: Working With Nature To Overcome Nature   98

Hugelkultur	100
Cover Crops	105
Fertilization	106
Soil Erosion	108
Weed Suppression	110
Companion Planting	114
Structure, Nutrient Accumulation, and Microclimate	115
Pest/Disease Repellent and Decoy	116
Pollinator Attractant	118
Research Permaculture	120

Urban and Suburban Food Security: Politics, Garden Plots, and Community-supported Agriculture   **122**
  Renting Garden Plots   125
    How To Start Your Own Community Garden 128
  Community-supported Agriculture: Buying From Local Farms   133
  Changing Politics: Fight For Self-sufficiency 136

Bee Garden: Preserving The World's Food Security   **141**
  Native Bees: The Underdogs   146

Dealing With Climate Change Debate and Food Security: Final Words   **153**

Introduction - A Dynamic World

2020 and climate change is still one of politic's most controversial topics. However, while the debate rages on discussing climate change and the solutions for it, people are wasting valuable time that could be spent preparing.

Now, more than ever, people need to strive for their own food security.

Food Security is the ability for people to have physical, economic, and social access to foods that satisfy not only their nutritional needs, but also dietary needs.

The West, particularly America and much of Europe, has seen exceptional food security across all spectrums (physical, economic, and social). For example, in the United States residents spend the lowest percentage of income on food compared to other countries, have the most physical access, and don't limit access based on social/political reasons. Most Americans don't have to wonder where their next meal is going to come from.

But what if that food security disappeared?

If there is one thing climate change has accomplished in the West, it is reminding people that the world is more dynamic than their daily lives lead them to believe. Out of touch with farming, people have lost grasp of how devastating erratic weather can be. The idea of a food shortage seems bizarre in lands where supermarkets are a dime a dozen. However, nature continues to bring a severe reality check with devastating hurricanes, record floods, droughts, wildfires and irregular winter weather.

Yes. A food shortage could just be another bad storm away. Maybe an abnormal drought. An unseasonal frost. Chains of natural and human-made events, if occurring in tandem, can cause devastation that current generations aren't familiar with. It's a reality people often fail to grasp until it is too late.

- In 2005, Hurricane Katrina devastated New Orleans and impacted millions in the U.S. Not only did physical access to food disappear, but years later, economic struggle still remains for those affected.

- In 2012, a record drought caused 1/6th of corn production in the U.S. to fail. The effect was seen throughout multiple parts of the economy as prices rose. Not significant enough to cause hunger but an example of what trouble worsening events could cause.

- In 2016, Hurricane Matthew brought record flooding to the Carolinas among other places, causing permanent damage to homes and structures that took anywhere from weeks to months to fix. Many people faced weeks without power and relied on provisions from federal agencies.

- In 2018, farmers in Northern and Central Europe faced a long drought that saw some areas receive 12% of normal rainfall. It resulted in states of emergencies and declarations of bankruptcy by some farmers.

- In 2019-2020, Australian wildfires raged across millions of acres, stressing the country and limiting transportation of goods, including food and supplies.

- Also in 2020, Indonesia experienced a flood resulting from the most rain in a 24-hour time frame since 1860s record keeping, destroying lives and displacing thousands.

This represents only a small fraction of climate and weather related events that have threatened food security. Phenomenons are often worse and occur more often in parts of Africa and Asia. In wealthy nations, people not directly affected by these occurrences usually only see the effects in the form of price increases. However, with climate change and devastating weather events increasing, it's likely only a matter of time before people are affected directly.

Thanks to global trade, low production can be offset by importing goods but importation is not ideal. It adds to the carbon footprint of goods and requires produce to be selected and picked for storage rather than quality. In addition, the more a country relies on importation, the more susceptible it is to foreign impacts, especially war.

All is not lost, though. Consideration of what to plant and invest in is more important than ever. Some plants prove to be more climate flexible and in a home setting, can be harvested reliably. This decision making and plant flexibility is why gardening at home is so crucial for maintaining food security.

Small Scale Gardening: A More Practical Way To Secure Food

Large farming operations have no choice but to follow the money. Shipping, yield, growth rate, and market price are all factors that must be considered. Resilience to the weather makes it way onto the list but there is much less that a large farm can do compared to a home-scale operation.

The basic precaution against weather involves choosing varieties that perform well and are specifically bred to resist drought, disease, pests, cold, etc. While this is extremely important, the weather isn't so simple and you often have multiple stresses that require direct intervention. Wind, hail, abnormal droughts, floods, and infestations can all be handled better when the operation is kept small. More labor intensive methods can also be used which increases the viability of growing organic. Small modifications to the growing area such as soil amendments are also more practical and allows for growing a polyculture rather than the monocultures seen in traditional farming.

Small-scale gardening allows you to do things that would be considered impractical on a larger scale.

Battling Drought: Amazing Abilities Of Mulch

Incorporating mulch into large-scale farming has been an ongoing battle for good reason. The practice helps reduce water loss, increase crop yield for many plants, reduce weeds, reduce erosion, regulate soil temperature, and provides slow-release nutrients while decomposing. However, organic mulch such as yard waste and wood chips, isn't practical for big farms.

While large farms can mulch using plastic or biodegradable strips, it doesn't compare to the benefits of using whole organic material. Not only do you lose the soil regenerative properties, but these man-made mulches can contribute to a large amount of production and trash as they must be replaced routinely.

Small garden mulching can be done sustainably and applied in sufficient quantities to reduce water loss rate by up to 80% in some soils.

Reducing Flood Damage: Raised Garden Beds

Opposite of droughts, but equally (if not more) devastating, are floods. Floods are what create some confusing statistics when it comes to a changing climate. An area can receive the same or even more annual rainfall, but still suffer from record-breaking droughts. The details are in the intervals between rainfall. Rain can come less often but when it does arrive, it drops tons of water.

While there is nothing that can guarantee crop protection from a major flood, building on raised beds in flood prone areas is incredible insurance.

Insurance that is yet again, impractical on a larger scale.

Raised beds will still take on a lot of water, but they drain much faster than planting at ground level. This is especially ideal when growing important root crops.

Wind Damage: Planting in the Proper Location

Wind damage is very underrated when it comes to farming problems. Not only can it kill transplants but also rip the leaves off of delicate shrubs and outright break trees. Some long-stem crops such as corn can see thousands of acres destroyed by destructive wind events like hurricanes, and lower crop yields from strong gusts.

In a field, there is practically nothing farmers can do to protect from wind. Plants require some wind to grow more sturdy, however, wind can also shred tender plants by blasting soil against them. For trees, stakes are commonly used but become less effective as the trees branch out and fruits.

At a small-scale there are several options to keep crops safe from high-winds and protect your food.

- **Planting wind-resistant trees or placing a fence to block the prevailing winds can solve most issues. You don't want to eliminate wind, just reduce its severity.**

- **Staking also becomes more practical when you have a few dozen trees rather than several hundred.**

- **Pruning plants to allow more air flow, reduce weak branches, and reduce** overall crown size can also prevent damage to many trees. A large crown (portion of plants above ground) can act like a parachute in strong winds. You may have experienced this when trying to grow a tree in a pot.

- Finally, for ultimate protection against winds, you can choose to grow in a sturdy greenhouse. This options is more limiting but completely eliminates wind damage unless it is a destructive event. Greenhouses can be damaged and require fixing.

Disease and Pests: Polyculture and Organic Gardening

It turns out that humans aren't the only ones who like warmer weather. As some areas see increased temperatures and warm Winters, they also experience an increase in crop pests and disease.

In 2016, the U.N. Food and Agriculture Organization (FAO) estimated that 20-40% of global food lost can be traced back to pest and disease outbreaks in crops.

A 2018 study predicts we will see a 10-25% increase in crop losses for 3 popular grains per degree of climate warming.

With numbers like that, it is easy to see how pests and diseases are a major concern for ongoing food security. Many people have forgotten the effects pests and diseases can have. It may have been some time ago, but I would like to remind people that the potato blight in 19th century Europe was responsible for over 1 million deaths. Keeping pests and diseases under control is a crucial goal world-wide.

Most people are under the impression that farmers just spray pesticides endlessly but that couldn't be further from the truth. Integrated Pest Management (IPM) is a very important aspect to farming and runs on the principle of only spraying chemicals when it is absolutely necessary.

The problem is that necessary times to spray are fairly often.

Large scale farms which are mainly monocultures can face complete devastation over the wrong decision of whether to spray or not. Pests and diseases can spread like wildfire because every plant is suitable for them. A terrible disease like Rice Blast, caused by a fungus infection, can cause a farm to lose 70% of their crop from it alone.

A lot of this major crop loss is due to using monoculture (planting only one type). While many will quickly say "just switch to a polyculture", large farms often don't have that freedom. Different plants require different planting methods, soil, nutrients, harvesting equipment, and knowledge. When you get into the dozens or hundreds of acres, you also need specialized equipment for each individual crop.

Monocultures are planted as a means of efficiency, not a lack of knowledge.

This risk for the sake of efficiency isn't required on the small-scale. A polyculture can be established and maintained much easier. This makes small farms/gardens more secure against pests and diseases. For example, if something wipes out your potatoes, you can still get your carrots.

Because of the small scale, regardless of the crop, most things can be harvested in a few hours using manual labor. In addition, some methods of pest management becomes more practical. Organic solutions for pests, such as mechanical removal and insecticidal soap, can work well enough to reach harvest time without any significant loss.

Chilling Hours and Erratic Freezes: Fruit Tree Dilemma

Not only are fruit trees susceptible to the problems previously mentioned but they also face two unique issues from warm winters and cold springs.

Many (not all) fruit trees have a unique period of dormancy that influence their fruiting. This dormancy is regulated by "chill hours", the number of hours exposed to cold temperatures. When a plant's chill hours are met after being dormant, it is then capable of breaking dormancy during a period of warm temperatures. Many fruit trees break dormancy by flowering and these flowers, which are expected to turn into future fruit, are usually all of the flowers for that year.

One problem arises when it has been cold enough for a tree to break dormancy and then it gets unseasonably warm enough for the tree to flower. If fruit trees begin the flowering process when there is still a danger of freezing, the cold has the potential of destroying most of the crop for that entire year.

Some trees are more resistant to this effect and can resist lower temperature than others when flowering, but no tree is immune. The stage of the flower bud also has an effect, where earlier stages are more resistant and full flower bloom is least resistant to cold.

The second problem is even more unique. Warm periods can cause fruit trees to flower when bees aren't completely active. Bees like it warmer than fruit trees need to flower. This decrease in pollination can cause loss of fruit yield, quality, and even shelf-life. Some crops can be estimated to lose up to 30-80% due to lack of pollination.

Bee pollination has been an ongoing battle even when separated from the effects of climate change. Adding more variables to successful pollination could prove to be devastating.

Much of this has made the risk of large-scale fruit tree farming too high. From climate to markets to time investment, fruit trees have become one of the riskiest crops to grow. If the climate becomes unfavorable for a certain fruit tree that could mean several years down the drain.

At the home scale, the scene is a little different. Not only can different tactics be used to protect trees from frost but you can also plant many different varieties.

Varieties of the same species can display different fruit yields, tolerance to frost, need for pollination, and length of harvesting period all under the same conditions. If you lose one variety to a late frost, it's possible another variety performs well with no problem.

In addition, as explained with polycultures, if you lose your fruit tree crop, you can buffer the loss with other harvests in the garden.

Relying on Large Farms is Risky

Put all of the above points together and it is easy to see how having your own small farm/garden is a smart idea. Natural events that can see larger operations devastated can be avoided on the smaller scale. With climate change predicted to exacerbate these issues, utilizing any land you have available to reinforce your food security has never been a better idea.

As you continue, you will find several ideas to help improve your property and also strong recommendations on what to grow based in the US. With the issue of fruit trees fresh in your mind, there's no better way to continue than by revealing easy and productive trees you can grow at home.

Climate Adaptable Fruit Trees (and Shrubs) For Self-sufficiency

You may be wondering why there is so much focus on fruit trees and not other plants. The reason for this is due to the nature of how we garden. Fruit trees are required to grow several years before getting a harvest while other garden plants are typically grown as annuals. Plants raised as annuals can be grown with much less regard to the Winter and Spring conditions, making them artificially climate adaptable.

Climate adaptable is the term I use to describe a plant that is able to be grown in a range of climates. This does not mean it can grow anywhere. Climate adaptable plants listed here focus more on surviving drought conditions, heavy rain, and/or hot weather while also being able to tolerate frost.

The criteria for this list is mainly focused on:

- **Productivity** - Being able to get a sizable harvest from a single plant.

- **Moderate Winter Survival** - Not killed by prolonged periods of cold and not critically susceptible to late freezes.

- **Drought/Flooding Resistance** - Able to survive short periods without rain and/or tolerant moist soil.

- **Susceptibility to Pests and Diseases** - Not bothered by many pests or susceptible to hard-to-treat diseases.

None of this is to say that growing fruit is effortless. Optimal fruit production will always require some degree of water consistency and knowledge of your growing season, but several trees are more forgiving than others. Also, keep in mind that even if a plant can survive drought it may cause a loss in fruit production for that year. With that being said, here is a short list of trees you should seriously consider growing.

Figs

First on the list is the almighty fig tree. Figs have a long history intertwined with human survival for good reason. Believed to have originated in Asia, then distributed throughout Europe, followed by California, Figs have already proven their ability to thrive in different areas. The delicious fruit tree is extremely fast-growing, drought tolerant, loves moist soil, and can produce hundreds of pints of fruit on mature trees.

In South America, where figs can grow vigorously, growers can expect over 100 lbs of fruit from a single tree. Although fig fruit spoils rapidly, it is perfect for making preserves that last throughout the Winter months.

However, the real gem about fig trees isn't how much they produce, but how their fruit ripens. Unlike most other non-berry fruit trees, figs do not ripen all at once. Once they start producing a sizable yield, you should be able to pick fresh fruit from Summer till frost.

Fig trees are relatively easy to grow and some people find it harder to kill them rather than grow them. Due to their aggressive root systems, they are able to recover easily even when cut down to the ground. Though some pest and disease can affect the plant, they can easily be managed with an organic treatment of neem oil. Figs are also one of the most responsive trees you can grow. They will "tell" you when something is wrong by yellowing and dropping leaves.

In regards to food security, Figs have a long history of helping both humans and animals survive. Different species of figs are responsible for reforesting lands in arid climates and providing a much needed source of plant life. The easily propagated nature of fig trees also make them one of the most important edible trees. You can literally start a fig forest using one plant. If you want a tree that can help provide security for an entire neighborhood, figs are definitely the way to go.

As more people become conscious of a changing climate I predict the popularity of figs to increase.

Grapes

Although not a tree or shrub, grapes are still one of the top producing perennials in the world. One vine can produce 20 pounds of high-sugar fruit and continue producing for over 50 years.

Grape vines, admittedly, aren't the easiest things to grow when it comes to disease and pests, but they are surprisingly tolerant to dry conditions. In fact, a lot of home grown vines meet their end due to too much care rather than not enough. The fast-growing vine doesn't like a lot of fertilizer or water (sounds amazing, right?). Instead, what grapes really need is a well-planned space and physical maintenance.

Sunlight, pruning, and good airflow makes grapes happy. While sunlight is important for the fruit, it is extremely important in helping to keep plants dry. Both the fruit and vegetation of grape vines grow clustered. This compactness can promote fungal growth and lead to diseases, which are the most troublesome aspect of growing grapes.

You are probably starting to question grapes at this point. Let me assure you that the troubles aren't as bad as they sound. Grape cultivation can be traced all the back to 6500 B.C. It is truly a crop that is ingrained in human civilization and will no doubt continue to hold influence.

If they could master growing grapes all the way back then, surely we can manage today with even more knowledge.

The main use of grapes throughout history has been wine and raisins. Both of these products preserve grapes and, in the case of raisins, can provide a source of fruit far after harvesting months. While I'm not an advocate of alcohol, dried fruit is another story. Food security is hardest during Winter and having a source of fruit during cold months is important for maintaining health.

Pomegranates

Many people are often surprised to learn that pomegranate trees are vigorous, highly productive, and drought tolerant. Some even consider the shrubs weedy because they grow so fast and sucker prolifically at the base.

The history of pomegranates like figs and grapes, dates far back and is intertwined with human civilization. The fruit has even gained religious significance in several different faiths. Native to the Middle East, the historic shrub has been distributed and grown successfully in nearly every continent. Despite not being a very common garden plant, the number of commercial growers has exploded in recent decades and continues to increase. Not only is there a market demand for pomegranates but the plant has proven itself to be a sturdy crop in the face of a changing climate. Pomegranate, however, are susceptible to too much water when fruiting. The swelling can cause the fruit to swell and burst.

Pomegranates are also one of the rare fruit trees that are sometimes planted for their unique flowers rather than the fruit. Interest in ornamental use has lead to horticultural research and development for varieties with more pronounced flowers. However, because these ornamental varieties do not produce good fruit, they have also seen a lack of desirability.

Beyond looking spectacular, pomegranate flowers provide a much needed food source for hummingbirds. Contrary to popular belief, hummingbirds are voracious insect feeders that use nectar for quick energy. Having these adorable birds in your garden can help keep pest populations under control.

Pomegranate seeds, which are the edible part of the fruit, freeze beautifully without any prep needed. They can prove to be a phenomenal source of vitamin C, something usually attributed to citrus fruit. One pomegranate, when the seeds are eaten whole, can provide 48% of the daily recommended intake for vitamin C. People with access to plenty of food and fortified meals have forgotten the importance of a balanced diet. One of the most infamous nutrition related diseases, scurvy, was diagnosed in a significant amount of people in 2002, Afghanistan. War and drought put pressure on local's already limited diet. The conditioned was actually diagnosed late by aid workers because scurvy had been very uncommon in established populations.

It's an unfortunate example of how food security can be disrupted by several events happening all at once.

Jujube

Jujube, also known as chinese date, is likely a new tree to many who read this. This popular, Asian tree is often regarded as a more heat-tolerant apple, though they are not related.

Originating from China, Jujube trees are somewhat of a mystery to me. They basically require no care and deliver loads of fruit but have not gotten much popularity here in America. They are a little more common thanks to popular gardening sources, but odds are, your everyday person isn't going to know about this fruit tree. In Asia, Jujube are very popular and used in everything from cooking to candies.

Jujube has one of the widest growing ranges of plants in this list. It can handle zones 5-10 with little difficulty, however the fruits do require a good amount of time to ripen. This can present a challenge to those living in areas with a short growing season. As for water, the tree is very drought tolerant. Even in hot, dry regions, the tree can grow vigorously and require annual pruning to maintain optimal harvesting height.

This is another excellent dried fruit candidate. Just four fruit can provide nearly 100% of vitamin C and it can reach a storage life of 6 to 12 months when stored properly. It's basically nature's vitamin C tablet. One interesting aspect about Jujube is that its fully ripened stage will actually dry on the tree and remain edible. The appearance of the dried fruit is where Jujube gets the name, Chinese date, but it is important to note that taste and texture resembles a dried apple rather than a date.

Jujube, like figs, also ripen in succession and are great for multiple harvests. If you prefer to eat fresh fruit, this trait is highly important. Planting multiple successive ripening fruit trees can promote large harvest of fresh fruit daily and still leave enough for preserving.

Persimmons

The two edible persimmons most commonly grown, American and Asian, have a long history in there respective regions. While the importance of American persimmon has largely been forgotten, Asian persimmon is still a prized fruit crop in China, Japan, and Korea.

Asian persimmons are considered to originate from China, which is also the largest producer of persimmon, by far. The trees are not just valuable crops but also beautiful ornamentals. During Fall and Winter, when most plants aren't doing anything, persimmons offer a brilliant orange display. One key difference between the history of Asian and American persimmon is that Asian persimmons have been highly cultivated. You will find more varieties that are more suitable for marketing. This is why most persimmon trees you will see for sale are an Asian variety.

American persimmons do not have the graceful appearance of Asian persimmons and typically bear much smaller fruit. This isn't a unique fault of the tree but rather a lack of breeding efforts. Most fruit trees you see today are a result of dedicated breeding. A focus on improving American persimmon has increased in past years but have a long way to go.

Native Americans valued persimmon trees for the bountiful fruit harvests and tree bark. Today the trees mainly see use as food for wildlife. The fall ripening nature of persimmons make them an important part of ecosystems.

When deciding which one to grow, it is important to note that American persimmons are true trees and will quickly grow beyond the size of most common fruit trees. For personal reference, I have both types growing and an American persimmon that has been cut down to a stump reached the same height as my 4-year-old Asian persimmon in one growing season. Asian persimmons can be expected to reach a height and spread of 30 feet if left alone. American persimmons can reliably reach heights of nearly 60 feet with 30 feet spread. For this reason, people with small properties are better off choosing an Asian persimmon variety.

That being said, American persimmons are a lot hardier than their Asian counterparts. Some can survive down to zone 4 while Asian varieties are normally rated to zone 7 lowest. I have also noticed that American persimmons can resist strong winds better. Both are fairly drought resistant and have little pest problems. However, the key determining factor for which persimmon you should grow is the fruit. All American persimmons that I know of have relatively small fruit and are astringent until fully ripened. Asian varieties, which have been bred to be commercially viable, have large fruit and can be found in non-astringent varieties.

It's also important to remember that persimmons can come in self-pollinating varieties, like Fuyu, or require a male and female plant, as seen with most American varieties. I'm not a fan of needing male plants to achieve pollination, since it takes up valuable garden space, but if you have a large property it is less of an issue.

Owari Satsuma Mandarin Citrus

Owari Satsuma mandarin citrus are the most cold-hardy "normal" citrus and can be planted as far north as zone 8. They are very productive and actually better tasting than many oranges you buy in supermarkets. When I say "normal", I mean these are the type that most people are accustomed to eating.

The observant reader may be wondering why an orange is included in a list for food security when our climate is getting warmer. "Eventually, everywhere will be able to grow oranges! Right?" Well, no.

The most devastating aspect of climate change (and fruit tree growing) is variability in weather. This entry is for those living in areas that are just on the border of citrus hardiness. Rather than taking a chance and planting citrus trees that could be killed by a cold snap, planting Owari Satsuma Mandarin citrus may prove a smarter decision.

Citrus trees are fantastic producers for hot climates and passing them over altogether is sacrificing a relatively carefree source of food. Citrus trees, depending on the variety and rootstock, are another crop that can reach over 100 pounds of produce from a single mature plant. The Owari mandarin is no exception. In addition, it sounds odd to those not familiar with citrus but they are another tree for Winter food. Mandarins are usually ready to harvest in December.

The nature of citrus trees falls in line with large rain events followed by long dry periods often seen with climate change. Citrus plants don't like for their feet to stay too wet. The common recommendation is only to water after they have dried from the previous watering which is what these events essentially achieve. With proper mulching, a citrus should see no problems making it through dry spells while retaining fruit. Giving a citrus unnecessary water actually does more harm than good. It is a common mistake people make when the trees self-thin the size of their crop.

Self-pollinating Pecan

America's native tree nut is also one of the most important. Rated for zones 5-9, pecans are a great source of needed fat and protein during the winter months. Native Americans recognized the value of pecans and used it for both food and trade.

It's not surprising that a tree linked with centuries of survival would retain its relevance. These southern nuts are nature's superfood and often go unappreciated in today's society where food is readily available. 1/2 cup of pecans has more energy(calories) than 6 cups of apples. That ratio is truly amazing and shows why it's so valuable as a crop. In the past a supply of nuts could mean the difference between surviving and starving.

Pecans certainly aren't the simplest plant to grow in this list. Being native, they are hardy in their rated zones but also have more pests than some of the other trees that originated from other countries. In addition, their large canopy makes them another tree that is susceptible to wind damage. For huge trees like pecans that become hard to treat as they get older, it's important to set them up for success at a young age. The three most important things you need to do when they are young are: place in the right location, make sure the roots are planted correctly, and train the tree for strong growth. Once you discover how to grow pecans, they will impress you with their vigor. Some varieties are able to put on six feet of growth every year. In a few years you will be rewarded with a productive tree and can enjoy the best part - eating it!

There are many ways to enjoy pecans. Eating it raw is delicious but I prefer another method. Roasting and blending my own pecan butter is an incredible experience. It also stores well in the fridge. Pecan butter, like peanut butter, can turn inexpensive bread into a tasty sandwich.

Talk about a smooth way to enjoy Winter.

Fruit Trees Are Just The Beginning

Putting fruit trees at the forefront is important because they need to be planted sooner rather than later. However, that isn't to say there aren't other important actions you should be taking to reinforce your food security. You may have noticed that the majority of the previous discussion was centered around drought and hot weather. That opens the questions as to what people in colder regions should do.

The next section will cover the importance of investing in a polytunnel to extend the growing season and the importance of roots crops.

Maintaining Food Security With a Short Growing Season

Northern regions often see amazing weather for growing food but it is short-lived. Warm Spring temperatures come late but sudden, which can affect seed germination, and cold temperatures arrive in Fall rather than Winter. In addition, the worst areas can experience frost almost any time of the year. Many trees that can tolerate the cold extremes often don't have enough time to mature fruit before the need to go dormant arrives and tender plants have to be chosen carefully. Luckily, there are high-value crops and methods available for those who want to do small-scale gardening in a short-growing season.

Polytunnels: The Cheaper Greenhouse

Those unfamiliar with gardening are probably used to hearing about greenhouses but less so about polytunnels. **Polytunnels,** also known as high tunnels, are semi-permanent structures, usually semi-circle in shape, that are covered in polythene(polyethylene) to act like greenhouses.

"What?! Plastic? You fool!"

Just hold up. I realize plastic is a controversial material and before we can continue further, a discussion must be had about the impacts of greenhouses, polytunnels, and farming.

When you start going up in size, the cost of a greenhouse begins to become too big of an investment for small growers. Not only that, but the odds of damage occurring is also greater. Many people have the perception that greenhouses are a build and forget style of construction but storms are commonly known to cause broken panels and even total collapse if not built properly.

Prebuilt-polytunnels and greenhouses also have a huge difference in price-to-size ratio. For this reference, I priced a polytunnel kit online vs a Walk-in greenhouse kit using polycarbonate frames. The Walk-in greenhouse actually covered less area but was near seven times the price of the polytunnel.

But what about the environment?

That is always a complicated question. Rather than justifying the use of plastic, I would like to provide insight on the benefits of growing your own produce and produce for your neighbors.

The two biggest reasons produce is shipped far is because they cannot be supplied locally year-round and there are manufacturers that offer the produce in convenient forms, usually frozen. Those tomatoes bought during Winter time likely aren't being grown in a greenhouse locally. They are probably coming all the way from somewhere warm, such as Florida.

That long transport certainly isn't a great model for a cleaner world, but it doesn't end there. In some areas, the drive to fresh food is quite far. To get fresh produce people can make trips to the store weekly, even daily. In addition, the produce in grocery stores are often packaged in plastic that doesn't get recycled or incinerated. That's certainly the wrong way to use plastic.

Polytunnels, on the other hand, not only puts the produce production at your doorsteps, but eliminates the use of plastic packaging. No more single heads of lettuce wrapped in plastic or tomatoes in cartons.

Extending access of the goods you grow to neighbors can offset more waste than what can be attributed to the polytunnel structure.

The plastic in polytunnels can also be thick and easy to keep track of. In 7 or so years, if there is a need to replace the plastic, it can be easily gathered and properly handled. This is a much better end than what is seen with plastic bags and packaging from supermarkets.

The message in the end is that there is a responsible use for all materials, including plastic. Growing without polytunnels or even conventional greenhouses is recommended where possible, but when it comes to food security, it's not so simple of a decision.

Benefits of a Polytunnel

So why even buy or build a polytunnel?

While you can control the conditions in a polytunnel, like a greenhouse, they are mainly used to create a microclimate. Microclimates are small-scale climates that are different from the surrounding area. They can be caused by artificial and natural factors.

Many people only think of temperature but a microclimate can also be centered on manipulating sunlight, wind, and moisture.

- **Sunlight** - Sometimes the only area for your garden is smack dab in the open sun. During peak heat, some crops that you are trying to grow year-round might not appreciate the harsh sunlight. To combat this, a common practice is putting shade cloth over the polytunnel or using shade cloth instead of the polythene.

- **Wind** - Discussed previously, wind damage can outright kill or damage tender plants. Polytunnels can protect against strong winds, while having the entrance left open for drafts and ventilation.

- **Moisture** - It's important to remember that greenhouses and tunnels are closed off to rain and need irrigation. While this sounds terrible, in cold climates, rainfall often does more harm than good. The slow evaporation can cause excess water to rot roots and promote diseases. Humidity can also be kept high, which aids in seed germination and growing plants that like it hot but not dry..

These managing features of polytunnels, along with the temperature increase, make them important for extending the growing season and having food year-round. Sometimes their use is related directly to their protective features rather than extending the season. Either way, they are valuable garden additions that should not be overlooked. Greenhouses can be attributed with the same benefits at a higher cost, but are considered by many as more attractive. There is no case to make against greenhouses if you can afford one, however, polytunnels provide a great alternative that is economically accessible for more people.

Potatoes: The Survival Crop

With a short growing season it's important to grow food that is dense in nutrients. Root/tuber crops are essential for this purpose and nothing shows it better than the history of potatoes.

Potatoes, and other root/tubers, are perhaps the most desired staple crops in their unprocessed state. Little changes about potatoes from when they are harvested to when they make their way to the pantry. They are mostly just cured for storage and ready to be eaten after cooking.

Potato curing and storage are the main challenges associated with harvested potatoes but that discussion should be left for qualified experts. Instead, I recommend people to prep potatoes by blanching and then freezing them. In fact, freezing potatoes is usually the only way most can store a large amount. People buy frozen potatoes all the time but seem to forget they can be frozen when it comes to storing their own.

Learning From Potato History

Unlike the fruit trees mentioned in this book, potatoes represent a true staple crop for many countries throughout history. The sole food is responsible for the survival of millions and when its production is hindered, it results in the fatal starvation of large populations.

Staple crops are plants that are grown and used in the diet of a large amount of people for the majority of their calories. Some other examples besides potatoes are rice, beans, and even bananas. These crops are often starchy and easy to grow in their respective regions.

Potatoes grew to fame in Europe but originate from Peru. Despite their South American origins, potatoes actually don't like it too hot, especially their roots. The Andes mountains, where Peru is located, are known for its varying weather, including snow and wetness. This is why the crop has been so successful in many parts of Europe and around the world. Potatoes had also gone through much cultivation by the local people by the time it was imported, making some varieties already suited for farming.

European conquest is sometimes attributed to the wide cultivation of potato crops. Although it took time for farmers to adopt the plant brought back by Spanish conquistadors, it signaled a revolution once it began to spread. Unlike the grain crops, potato crops were difficult to ruin and produced a better return in poorer soil. Europe's peasant population had a highly nutritious crop to match their demanding pace and the cases of famine decreased dramatically, especially when compared to the rest of the world.

The potato and its history is a testament to what industrial farming can accomplish, freeing people from farm work and allowing their manpower to be placed elsewhere. However, the very same crop also serves as a cautionary tale of what happens when you place your food security in the hands of a true monoculture.

Nearly all of the potato that was planted throughout Europe were clones of each other. In the 19th century, when the water mold *Phytopythora infestans* was introduced, destruction of the monoculture happened too quickly for Europeans to adapt. Over the course of a few years, several million acres of potatoes were lost to potato blight and over a million people starved as a result. Ireland experienced the worst of the blight and emigration from the country skyrocketed as a result.

While the great famine in Ireland seems like a forgotten period in history that humans have moved past, there is actually a risk of similar events happening again in many countries. Monocultures are still vastly used in agriculture. Global trade along with changing climates can see new pests and disease emerging. Stress from harsh weather and pests can cause large crop failure spanning across several nations. While wealthy countries are particularly safe from famine due to diverse food sources, government programs, and trade, it is not something to take lightly. Keep in mind that most recent large-scale famines also involve some political aspect. If you really want to be in control of your food security, establishing your own diverse crops is an important step.

You might even want to consider some less traditional crops to grow...

Exploring New Crops: The Usefulness Of Varieties and Foreign Plants

Traditional crops may not be the best in the face of a changing climate. Some would consider many of the things grown today as "luxury crops". True luxury crops are crops grown for use other than maintaining human life. Some would argue that because we end up eating fruits and vegetables, none of them fall into the category, but I disagree. I prefer to extend the definition to include growing crops that require heavy inputs when there is no need. Nothing describes this better than the American favorite, tomatoes.

Fresh tomatoes are desired year-round, including Winter. Although there is an abundance of frozen, dried, and canned tomato available, people insist on having a fresh fruit. This demand is met with heavy supply. Tomato growing is largely sourced to locations with high temperatures year-round but often inadequate growing conditions. Without the heavy irrigation and pesticide use, it would be hard to get a reliable harvest of tomatoes in these areas. People don't see this side of farming and just think the tomato plant simply belongs in any garden.

Don't be fooled.

Having a garden to be more food secure means little if that garden isn't easy to sustain. Market familiarity has conditioned many gardeners into believing some plants are garden essentials, such as tomatoes, but you may be setting yourself up for failure striving to grow them. Instead, I urge you to explore the wide range of fruits and vegetables and find what grows best, even if you aren't accustomed to it.

Ways to Find New Varieties to Grow

Plants can differ in many ways. From the obvious (different species), to the not so obvious (different varieties). It's important to find what species you want to grow and then see if there are varieties of that species that will do particularly well in your area.

Varieties are the main way people find new crops. Gardeners who can't live with the idea of not growing a plant will look for the best version. This can work very well. Varieties can be bred to improve disease resistance, pest resistance, heat tolerance, cold tolerance, drought resistance, fruiting time, yield, flavor, flowering, and growth habit. These results are incredible but not always the answer.

Sometimes your conditions are so unfavorable that another species is the only sustainable option. This is usually seen in areas with a high concentration of crop specific pests or disease. For example, if you have issues with late potato blight it might serve better to find a different tuberous crop, like sweet potatoes, which is a different species and less vulnerable.

Online is the best way to find new varieties to grow and substitute with. Professional garden businesses organize their seeds and plants so that you can sort through different varieties for each species. Normally, these sites will note the trait that a variety has been bred for. Usually it is either yield or disease resistance as these are important commercial traits.

Beyond online garden stores, people in forums can offer their own experience with certain varieties and may recommend ones that you wouldn't have heard of otherwise. This is my favorite method of research since garden businesses often only mention the positive traits of their varieties. However, forums can often be sparse in specific information.

To get the most detailed look at the popular varieties for your area you should look up

articles by your state cooperative extension or research university. These resources not only tell you the best plants to grow but also provide key considerations and details specific to the region. The more detailed profiles will also give expected yield and harvest time for many crops.

Thinking Outside The Box: Foreign Vegetables and Fruits

As I mentioned briefly, if a specific variety isn't suitable, you need to pick a whole different species. If that's the case, try thinking outside the box and see if there are some exotic crops you'd like to try that fits your growing area.

Exotic crops might be a little redundant since many crops originated from other countries, but the common ones have seen large breeding efforts to make them unique to our area. Those same practices are sometimes carried out in other countries and the results are slowly brought to the US. In addition, plant explorers are constantly on the search for heirloom plants in other countries that might be suitable for US gardens.

Several online garden centers have plenty of these available for you to experiment with, but my favorite has been **Rareseeds.com**

Rareseeds.com, ran by Baker Creek Heirloom Seeds, is a great place to find unusual plants that can possibly do well in your garden where most others fail. I love looking at the selection and thinking of future possibilities. Not just the possibility of finding something new, but actually developing something new. Plenty of the rare plants have not gone through extensive breeding. It is quite possible to take a new species and selectively breed it to create your own strain for your growing conditions. This process is one of the ways several famous garden varieties were developed.

It's important to remember that you should only buy seeds from a certified seller. There are laws that need to be followed when it comes to bringing in plants from another country. In addition, many scams exist trying to sell common seeds as unique varieties. Seeds from an unreputable seller may even be an invasive weed that ruins your garden.

Breeding a plant to suit your conditions is possible but time consuming, so what should you do when time is of the essence? Once again, we need to take advantage of working on a small scale using some crafty gardening techniques.

Lost Gardening Techniques: Working With Nature To Overcome Nature

While industrial agriculture is rather new to human history, small-scale farming has been around for a long time. As one can imagine, growers developed several techniques to deal with the plethora of problems one can encounter when trying to produce food. From droughts to pests, great agricultural minds already got their hands dirty and passed on the knowledge of how to overcome such troubles when changing crops is not an option. Mulching survived the test of time and earned its place even in industrial farming but some other techniques that aren't widely adopted are **hugelkultur, cover crops, and companion planting**.

Hugelkultur

Hugelkultur, or Hill Culture, is a farming technique originating from Germany that involves the use of tree wood and debris to create modified planting beds. These planting beds, which were rather large in history, are first dug out and then filled with wood/soil layers until a large mound is formed. Large wood on the bottom and smaller wood higher up. Afterwards, it is covered with a final layer of soil and allowed to sit over winter or even for a full growing season. **Some people like to use manure or compost because the decomposition can use available nitrogen.** As the tree material breaks down it acts like a sponge and absorbs a large amount of water. The water it holds becomes a slow-release source for plants during dry periods.

In addition, it improves the soil and provides many nutrients.

While in the past hugelkultur was done using deep trenches and large pieces of wood, you don't have to go to such extreme lengths. An easier and safer way to benefit from this practice is to use it when building raised beds.

Using raised beds for hugelkultur has many benefits.

- **It adds cheap fill to large beds, drastically reducing your cost.**

- The decaying wood holds and slowly release moisture which can reduce the need to water.

- Decaying organic matter encourages worms to enter the garden bed, helping to enrich the soil.

- Not having to dig into the ground eliminates the risk of hitting dangerous utility lines.

- It provides a wasteless way to dispose of old wood and Fall leaves.

If dry weather is an issue hugelkultur is a great way, along with mulch, to keep soil moisture levels consistent. Crops that do not like inconsistent water can see much better performance using this technique. For best results, use raised beds at least 2 feet high. Also, NEVER use potting mix for a raised bed garden. Potting mix dries out extremely fast. I use a mix of composted cow manure and peat moss followed by mulch with leaves or straw. I also like to add a layer of shredded leaf mold (decaying leaves) to serve as a quick-acting sponge and prevent water from draining too fast. However, because my mixture contains no soil, it does require replenishing with the level gets too low.

Maybe even a raised bed is too large of a step for you. If that's the case,you can practice the hugelkultur method using potted plants. Plant pots are infamous for drying out too fast, sometimes needing multiple waterings a day. Placing organic matter at the bottom can bring all of the benefits of hugelkultur where it is needed most. Keep in mind that because pots have less mass, extra nitrogen is needed in the beginning and it is better to start with semi-decayed material rather than fresh.

As a final note, **hugelkultur beds can become nests for wood loving pests like carpenter ants and termites**. If you have such pests in your area it may be better to avoid using large wood and try alternatives such as leaf mold or wood chips.

Cover Crops

Cover crops are plants grown in the off-season or during crop rotation. Rather than being harvested for their vegetation or fruit, these plants are valued for their ability to improve the planting area. The use of cover crops has seen its ups and downs since its first mass implementation in the US by George Washington. The first president, who was also a farmer, saw the value of taking time to care for the soil. It was regarded as a necessary step in farming.

Some of the numerous benefits of cover crops are fertilization, reduced soil erosion, improved water retention, weed suppression, and possibly better yields during drought conditions.

Fertilization

It probably sounds odd growing a plant in a space to fertilize it but it's all about how nutrients in soil and plants work. Cover crop fertilization usually works in two ways. Nitrogen-fixing crops add nitrogen when incorporated and nutrient-scavenging crops store nutrients in their roots to prevent them from washing away.

Legumes are used as nitrogen fixers, while grasses and brassicas are used to capture nutrients. It's important to remember that the nitrogen fixing nature of legumes is reliant on a symbiotic fungal relationship. You may need to inoculate your garden to see results or make sure to buy pre-inoculated seeds.

This ability to grab nitrogen out of the air and sequester it, is extremely important for self-sufficient gardening. Unless you raise animals or decide to use your own body waste, nitrogen can be had to come by without relying on an outside source. Minimizing inputs should always be a goal of a grower, whether small or large.

The first year of using a cover crop, you shouldn't expect to meet all of your fertilization needs but each successive year should provide better results. These are called the soil building and maintenance phases. The building stage should see an influx of organic material followed by soil analysis every year. Once nutrient levels are high, you can then rely on just the cover crop for organic material if you wish. This is the maintenance phase.

Unlike compost and regular mulch, cover crops truly improve soil over time by building roots through it and keeping soil fungi alive between planting seasons.

Soil Erosion

The spacing of crops and lack of growth during the off season can leave soil exposed. This bare soil becomes dry, lifeless matter with nothing to stop it from eroding due to wind and water. The most infamous case of this was the 1930s Dust Bowl.

Improper farming practices, drought, and wind caused over 850 million tons of topsoil to be lost from erosion. Top soil is the most important layer of soil for plants because it contains most of the nutrients they need. The top layer of organic matter also increases water infiltration, allowing crops to benefits from even brief amounts of rain.

If you are doing in-ground farming and aren't protecting your soil you can be making your crop less drought-tolerant as a result.

The roots of cover crops hold soil in place while the leaves acts as living mulch and add back to the top soil when cut down. This is a great DIY way of mulching your garden. Rather than spending money and transportation costs bringing in mulch, you can produce your own from seed.

Weed Suppression

Weeds love bare soil more than anything. Either you plant something in the soil or mother nature will.

Most cover crops are highly competitive with plants of similar height and can grow densely. Many, like clover, are actually consider weeds in other settings. The aggressive nature plays a lot into which plants are chosen as cover crops.

However, weeds are weeds for a reason. Cover crops need to be planted and established before the main weeds in your garden. This means, for the best effect, you will have to research when the weeds germinate and what crop will germinate before it. In addition, your soil nutrient levels can affect cover crop performance. Not surprising, legumes can grow better than other cover crops in soils with low nitrogen.

Ultimately, weed suppression is another benefit for an in-ground garden that can directly improve the health of plants you grow. Weeds can severely reduce your garden's drought tolerance, increase the need for nutrients, and promote the colonization of pests. Weeds are one of the greatest barriers to farming around the world and not something that should be taken lightly. If you are planning a small-scale farm and want to be as organic as possible, cover crops are a great tool for weed control.

All of this isn't to say that cover crops are all good and no bad.

Cover crop use on a large-scale is an intricate process. There is a wealth of knowledge that should be understood before trying to apply this technique in a large setting. Like I mentioned, some of the crops can be considered weeds themselves if you do not manage them appropriately. Having to incorporate cover crops can also be a challenge and unwanted task for many people. It's important to consider all of the pros and cons before seeding an area.

Companion Planting

Companion planting is an old technique centered on grouping plants that benefit from being together. Its use in history is most famously known in America with the Three Sisters method utilized by Native Americans.

The Three Sisters where maize, squash, and beans. In simple terms, maize was grown to act as a support for the beans, the beans provided nitrogen for surrounding plants, and the squash acted as a living mulch, retaining moisture, shading out weeds, and even protecting from deer.

As you can see, careful consideration can create a garden with synergy. You may have even noticed that companion planting shares similarities with cover crops. The rising interest in companion planting has led to many beneficial plant pairings. Typically a pairing focuses on at least one of the following: **structure, pest/disease repellant, pest decoy, nutrient accumulation, microclimate, or pollinator attractant**.

Structure, Nutrient Accumulation, and Microclimate

These three qualities were addressed with the Three Sisters method. Structure almost always refers to providing support for a vining plant. Nutrient accumulation is like I discussed with cover crops, however, doesn't have to be confined to agricultural plants. Plants with deep tap roots and abundant vegetation can be "harvested"(cut leaves but keep plant) and used as chop and drop mulch to provide nutrients from a depth in the soil other plants can't reach. As for microclimates, a plant can either provide shade or act as a windbreak for more delicate plants near it. For a windbreak trees and shrubs are used most often.

Pest/Disease Repellent and Decoy

Sometimes if you are trying to grow something that is susceptible to pests and diseases it can be combated with specific companion plants. Repellents can be both physical and chemical. Physical repellents mainly includes plants with prickles or large thorns that can deter large animals. Chemical repellent relies on special compounds in a plant to ward off pests. Many of these plants can be identified by their strong scents. Some plants, like Chrysanthemum, contain chemicals effective enough to be used as an actual insecticide.

Pest decoys are exactly what they sound like. Some pests can be encouraged to leave your garden plants alone if you give them something else they prefer. Exactly what plant should you give them? The answer to that varies. Each pest likes something different. You will find that companion planting is a lot of trial and error based on personal experiences. A lot of knowledge about companion plant pairing has been gained from gardeners over many years.

Pollinator Attractant

Use of companion plants as pollinator attractants is probably the most popular and easy-to-verify use. We've all seen bees go absolutely crazy for some plants more than others. Placing these in the garden is a great way to ensure you get proper pollination. Deciding which plants need the most help can require a little bit of observation and research. For instance, I realized that bees don't really go after my tomato flowers but love squash flowers. Naturally, I was curious and investigated for a reason. Apparently, honey bees don't pollinate tomatoes but large ones, like bumblebees, do.

Thus, I researched for flowers that bumblebees specifically like and planted them around my tomato bed.

As you can see, there are several benefits that working with nature can provide. It not only creates a sustainable way to be food secure, but also allows you to grow some plants that would otherwise have trouble in the area.

Research Permaculture

All of these practices are tied to a method of gardening known as Permaculture. Permaculture is the cultivation of plants and use of animals in a system that mimics the natural ecosystem. Permaculture design seeks to minimize both inputs and waste using natural methods. For example, chickens can serve to eat pests, provide compost, till soil, and provide food. The "waste" from raising chickens fuels the garden and essentially stays in a closed system. Your cover crop can even be converted to chicken feed so you don't have to purchase any or as much. This and the methods above are just small examples of permaculture techniques. Because an entire book can be (and have been) dedicated to the topic of permaculture, I highly suggest exploring it further by acquiring the text of experts on the topic.

Urban and Suburban Food Security: Politics, Garden Plots, and Community-supported Agriculture

All of the information previously provided works on the assumption that you have sole-ownership of land to cultivate, but many people aren't so fortunate. The fact is most people live in urban and suburban communities. Obviously, apartment renters don't have free reign over the land but even homeowners can find their hands tied due to an HOA (Homeowners Association) or zone ordinance.

These regulations are a major threat to food security and make people susceptible to one of the major causes of hunger, politics.

I won't say that working around these issues is easy but I will say they are worth the fight and extra work involved. Living in an apartment shouldn't keep you from seeking out fresh food and laws against gardening shouldn't make you give up the fight.

Renting Garden Plots

Perhaps the easiest way to overcome your barrier to gardening is seeking out a garden plot for rent. Garden plot rentals are seeing increasing popularity and may be easy to find in your area. Plot rentals often come from farmers looking to monetize unused land or the city itself but sometimes small private landowners also rent out land for use.

Garden plots are usually either self-managed or community-managed. This has both its pros and cons. A self-managed plot requires more work and responsibility, but you have the freedom to plant what you want (to an extent). Community-managed plots sometimes have central members that decide what is planted and the community just works together for a shared harvest. Sometimes community gardens will provide both self-managed plots for rent along with community-managed plots.

Plots or farmland provided by farmers are generally larger than what cities and small landowners offer. These plots can be several acres large and often require you to have some farming experience. Many people seek rental farmland when they want to work on a large-scale but don't have the capital to buy land. Depending on the land and area, leasing farmland can be relatively cheap or very expensive. Farm owners also reserve the right to decide what you can and cannot use their land for. This method is typically only practical for those who plan on receiving some monetary returns from the operation.

If you can't find any garden plots to rent in your area, it won't hurt to ask local communities if they would be interested in transitioning some of their land into garden space. Churches are usually happy to start their own community gardens as long as there is an organized plan and enough support. A friend or family member might also be willing to let their property be used as a garden. If you go this route, however, it's important that you are serious about it. No one is going to be happy about an abandoned garden on their land.

How To Start Your Own Community Garden

1. Before going through a lot of trouble and committing time, it's important to see if creating a garden is allowed and if the land involved requires special legalwork like public liability insurance or signage requirements. Check with your town's planning department and also the HOA if you have one.

2. See how much support a community garden would receive. Go through your social networks and find out who would be interested in contributing to the garden. Decide if you want a community garden that

provides food in bulk or one that allows others to grow their own food in assigned lots.

3. Decide the name of your garden and create a list of main contributors. Main contributors will serve as a committee for the community garden and should only be people who express a desire to help with the garden long-term. The committee should get together, determine goals for the garden, and assign responsibilities on a volunteer basis.

4. The best community gardens and the ones that receive the most support have a goal in mind. Decide if you want you garden to

work with a specific goal in mind. If so, be sure to spread the word to gather even more support from businesses that are willing to donate materials.

5. Find someone who is willing to host a community garden with a site that is suitable for growing. Check to make sure it has adequate sunlight, uncontaminated soil, access to water, area for parking, and room to bring in loads of material. Before solidifying your space and making changes, it's best to check with your city again. Always be transparent with the landowner in any changes and activities you plan to do.

6. Once everything is approved, get with your committee and plan your garden on paper to stay organized. Decide the size of plots, location, paths, storage, space for material loads like compost, and fencing to protect from unwanted guests.

7. Create rules for your garden, how plots are assigned, if a fee is involved, who handles dues, etc. Rules may not be fun but they are essential to long-term success. Dues can also encourage people to take the plots seriously and not abandon them without notice. Rules should displayed on site and also handed out in writing to new members who rent a plot.

8. Once your garden is up and running, create an online presence that documents seasonal progress and events. Making other people aware of your community garden can keep member levels steady and the garden thriving for years. After your garden has documented success it can also be easier to garner support from businesses. Landscaping companies looking for good PR opportunities are especially useful as they can provide some of your most expensive materials, like mulch, for free.

Community-supported Agriculture: Buying From Local Farms

Sometimes a garden plot and even your own community garden are out of the question. The next best method for food security is helping local farmers maintain their place in the community. This can be accomplished by participating in their CSA program or buying from the local farmer's market.

CSA programs are programs sometimes offered by farmers that allow you to pay in advance to receive a certain amount of their harvests. Usually the produce you recieve is random but they try to inform you what will be growing for the season.

This option can be limited depending on where you live, with rural areas having more options.

While many people have the impression that CSA's are expensive, they can save you money in the long-run if you are one to eat fresh produce every week. The cost structure is different for each one but is generally developed for weekly, seasonal, or annual subscriptions. Many of the farmers with this program also participate at farmer's markets and give discounts to CSA members.

Because they must have a variety of produce, CSA farmers operate using polycultures. In addition to fruits and vegetables, a large amount of CSA farmers also provide other goods including free-range meat, honey, mushrooms, and flowers.

You will find that they are often leading the charge in organic growing and sustainable agriculture.

Supporting your local farmers is a great way to indirectly keep food security high in your area. By rewarding their practices, it can encourage others to start their own CSA ventures throughout the country. If you want to find a CSA near you, try searching online or visiting your farmer's market. Ask around and even if none of the vendors have a program in place, it could give them the idea to start one.

Changing Politics: Fight For Self-sufficiency

Even CSA's and Farmer's markets aren't foolproof. Maybe there are none close to you or maybe you are intent on growing something local farmers don't offer. Either way, if that's the case and gardening in your area isn't allowed, the only option is to either move or fight the laws.

A legal battle is anything but easy, but, it's a fight worth having in my opinion.

In 2013, a Florida couple faced an ordinance violation that called for the removal of their front yard garden. The couple, Hermine Ricketts and

Tom Carroll, fought a battle for six years that gained national attention. The results of that battle? In 2019, the Florida governor signed a bill that voided all ordinances that prevented home owners from growing produce on their lawns.

It's both a heart-warming and heart-breaking story. The fight for self-sufficiency shouldn't be so difficult, it shouldn't even exist but it does in many areas. Depending on where you live, a similar fight may be waiting for you. In that's the case, there are ways to increase your chances of achieving change. These recommendations apply more to government policy rather than Home Owner Associations.

Some HOA's have the power to foreclose homes and you should know the risks before trying to oppose them.

- Start with city meetings or HOA board meetings. Bring the problem to the attention of friends, family, neighbors and even strangers. Facebook is a great way to get local support and gardening communities on sites like Reddit can make issues go viral. I highly recommend trying to talk with HOA members first if that is the source of your issue. A large legal battle could be avoided by participating in meetings and politely asking for change or an exemption. HOA rules are also tricky since you are, in essence, contracted to follow them.

- Start a petition and get support to advocate democracy. Politicians feel more pressure when there is a petition to hold against existing policies. Many politicians are also looking for any way to gain new supporters and petitions are good guides for them.

- Pitch your story to reporters, both online and local. Green politics are high priority stories for media. Your situation could earn a spot on a national platform which further moves politicians to act.

- Search for an advocacy group to fight the fight with you. Legal battles are intimidating and often times costly, however, advocacy groups are not strangers to legal procedures. These groups can help perform the necessary steps to achieve the change you are looking for.

- Don't lose steam. The fight for change only stays alive as long as you keep it alive. It's very common for legal battles to extend over several years. Keep people updated and don't let the fight die down, especially locally.

These recommendations aren't going to guarantee change but can certainly help. **Food security means also being secure from politics that affect your ability to take survival into your own hands.**

Bee Garden: Preserving The World's Food Security

I get it. Some people reading this possibly don't like the idea of growing food or fighting government policies and the trouble it brings. Although I highly recommend doing so, there is no shame in choosing not to.

If you do forego your own small-scale food production, I would urge you to at least consider building an ornamental garden that supports bee populations. Why bees? BEE-lieve it or not, bees are actually incredibly important to the entire world's food security but have been facing many hardships over the years.

Bees, especially honey bees, are crucial for the world's pollination of food crops. An estimated 35% of crops rely on bees for pollination. That's a shocking number but even more jarring is that nearly all of the bees used for industrial pollination in the US are owned by just 5% of beekeepers. Much like industrial farming, the majority of pollination has been placed in the hands of a few large operations.

As honey bee colonies continue to experience major decline and the costs of restoring them increases, there is an increasing likelihood that we will see many large-scale beekeepers either leaving the business or charging a price that many growers cannot afford. Honey bee colonies experience the most death during Winter making it impossible to restore them before some of the high-value crops flower in Spring. The limited number of bees reduces the number of clients beekeepers can serve. This decline in income potential along with increase in maintenance cost has been devastating for the business and orchardist-relations.

Luckily, bees and their preservation has received global recognition. More hobbyist beekeepers are popping up every year and advocates are pressuring for government change. However, these efforts still fail to keep the honey bee population from declining. Climate, pesticides, habitat loss, disease, and mite infestations are proving too difficult to combat. As a result, to preserve food security, there has been greater discussion on exploring and promoting native bee populations.

Native Bees: The Underdogs

If you remember my tomato example, it's one of many cases where honey bees actually aren't the best bee for the job. Many crops are pollinated by one or several of the many thousand bee species roaming the country.

So how did honey bees get the spotlight? Well, quite a few reasons.

Honeys have four qualities all-in-one that make them exceptional. They are one of the few bee species that actually make honey, they make hives which allows them to be transported, they travel extremely far to find food and they are fairly docile which makes them safe to handle.

On a large-scale all of those traits are necessary. Even the honeymaking aspect allows beekeepers to cross-monetize their hives and offset some costs. However, small growers focused on food only need the pollination. Hive transportation isn't necessary and honey is only a plus.

That means, on a small scale, attracting native bees and building a habitat for them can possibly serve the same job as having a honey bee colony. It is reported that tomato growers get a 50% increase in yield from regular bumble bee pollination. Certainly nothing to laugh at.

Because native bees don't always live in a hive your ornamental garden can serve as a necessary habitat that helps growers close by in your area. Small-scale growers are often trying to maximize production space. Their areas are too often disturbed to support bee populations that do not build hives.

Building a space for native bees can be a little challenging. Some people think planting flowering plants is enough, but that couldn't be further from the truth. Here are some guidelines to optimize your area for native bees.

1. Research local bees in your area and determine what food they like and how they nest.

2. Plan your space carefully. Constantly disturbing the area to make changes can drive away or even kill bees that have made a home. Know exactly how you want your garden and try to focus more on perennial plants, rather than annuals.

3. Commit to keeping your garden free of pesticides and herbicides. Bees are highly susceptible to residue from chemicals. If any are used, never spray them on a flowering plant.

4. If possible, designate your own conservation area where the ground can be left undisturbed. Many bee species borrow

into the ground to nest. Bee "hotels" should also be placed in these areas to provide an additional habitat.

5. Switch to mowing every two weeks. A Biological Conservation study found that lawns mowed every two weeks showed higher bee populations and diversity than lawns mowed every week or every three weeks.

6. Add a water source to your garden. Be sure to add a floating surface that bees can land on to drink. Bees not only need water for themselves but also the rest of the hive. Entomologists estimate that on hot days,

bees can collectively bring a gallon of water back to the hive for other uses.

7. Plant masses of flowering plants that native bees enjoy. Don't be too concerned if the plant itself isn't native, as long as it isn't invasive. Your garden should provide year-round flowers, especially for late Winter and Early spring.

Turning your space into a bee habitat is a rewarding and less intensive way to reinforce food security. Your actions can encourage others to follow suit. The difference it would make if everyone's property was filled with oceans of flowers would be tremendous. It is a great example of how we can provide for ourselves by providing for others.

Dealing With Climate Change Debate and Food Security: Final Words

In the end, climate change debate can be hard to deal with. Some get frustrated and scared by the lack of action and others approach the issue with a degree of skepticism. I believe the majority of people at least agree that climate and weather are a threat to our immediate well-being. Regardless of your position, no one can argue against the importance of being prepared for the worst and reinforcing your safety and the safety of your family.

You might think there is time to wait but weather events are often unexpected and capable of happening every year. Roads can get flooded, stores can get caught in disasters, and dangerous conditions for driving can last days or even weeks. While famine is unlikely, reduced food security is a realistic possibility. Having your own source of fresh produce resistant to weather events, can keep you prepared for some of the worst times.

I hope you enjoyed this short read and that it has motivated you to start even the smallest of gardens. Just remember, if you had planted a fruit tree last year it could be providing fruit for you this year.

Thank you for reading!